Get Crafting for Your

BUSY BUNNY

by Ruth Owen

BEARPORT
PUBLISHING

Minneapolis, Minnesota

CREATE!

Library of Congress Cataloging-in-Publication Data

Names: Owen, Ruth, 1967- author.
Title: Get crafting for your busy bunny / Ruth Owen.
Description: Create! books edition. | Minneapolis, Minnesota : Bearport
   Publishing Company, [2021] | Series: Playful pet projects | Includes
   bibliographical references and index.
Identifiers: LCCN 2020039110 (print) | LCCN 2020039111 (ebook) | ISBN
   9781647476595 (library binding) | ISBN 9781647476663 (ebook)
Subjects: LCSH: Rabbits—Equipment and supplies—Juvenile literature. |
   Handicraft—Juvenile literature.
Classification: LCC SF453.2 .O94 2021 (print) | LCC SF453.2 (ebook) | DDC
   745.592—dc23
LC record available at https://lccn.loc.gov/2020039110
LC ebook record available at https://lccn.loc.gov/2020039111

For more information, write to Bearport Publishing, 5357 Penn Avenue South, Minneapolis, MN 55419. Printed in the United States of America.

CONTENTS

GET CRAFTY WITH YOUR BUNNY

If you enjoy crafting and love making life cozier, tastier, and more exciting for your pet rabbit, then this is the book for you! Discover four projects that will give you and your furry, long-eared pet hours of bunny fun.

Home Sweet Home

This homemade bunny bed is cozy and eco-friendly. It lets you **recycle** an old sweater and unwanted fabric scraps!

Pet Snacks and Treats ▶

Celebrate a bunny birthday, adoption day, or other special day with this yummy carrot cake treat for your pet.

Time to Play

Build this cardboard **maze** and keep your bunny's body and brain healthy and **active**. Your furry friend will have lots of fun **foraging** for food inside!

◀ Dress It Up

Make this carrot-shaped hat and dress up your best bunny buddy as a cone-shaped crunchy treat.

Have Fun and Be Safe

Crafting for your busy bunny can be lots of fun. But it's important that both you and your rabbit stay safe by following these top tips for careful crafting.

- Always get permission from an adult before making the projects in this book.

- Read the instructions carefully, and ask an adult for help if there's something you don't understand.

- Be careful when using scissors, and never let your rabbit touch or play with them.

- Keep any glue where your rabbit can't sniff, lick, or touch it.

- When your project is complete, recycle any extra paper, cardboard, or packaging. If you have leftover materials, keep them for a future project.

- Clean up when you've finished working.

- Remember! Some rabbits do well with petting and playing. But others seem to prefer only a little attention from their humans.

Never force your rabbit to do something it seems unhappy to do.

A COZY BUNNY BED

No matter where your bunny lives, it needs a safe shelter. And when it's time to sleep, this cozy, bunny-friendly bed will be a perfect **accessory** for your rabbit's space.

You will need

- An old sweatshirt or sweater
- A large needle
- Thin yarn in a color that matches the sweater
- Sewing pins
- Scissors
- Old, clean T-shirts, socks, bath towels, or dish towels
- An adult helper

You need to pin and stitch along the dotted line.

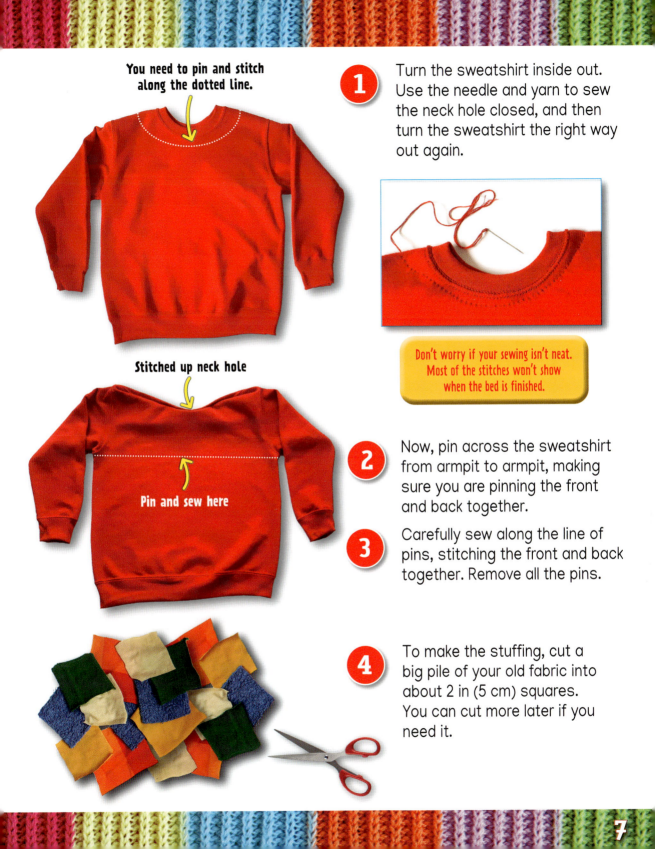

1 Turn the sweatshirt inside out. Use the needle and yarn to sew the neck hole closed, and then turn the sweatshirt the right way out again.

Don't worry if your sewing isn't neat. Most of the stitches won't show when the bed is finished.

Stitched up neck hole

Pin and sew here

2 Now, pin across the sweatshirt from armpit to armpit, making sure you are pinning the front and back together.

3 Carefully sew along the line of pins, stitching the front and back together. Remove all the pins.

4 To make the stuffing, cut a big pile of your old fabric into about 2 in (5 cm) squares. You can cut more later if you need it.

5 Next, fill the body of the sweater with stuffing to make the center part of your bunny bed.

Stuffed the center part of the bed

6 Once the center of the bed is stuffed, tuck in the bottom edges of the sweater and pin along the edge. Next, carefully sew up the join, or overlap, and then remove the pins.

7 Now, fill the sleeves and the top part of the sweater with stuffing. Keep filling this section until it can't fit any more stuffing. This will be the sides of the bed, so it's fine to stuff it until it's firm.

8 Wrap the sleeves of the sweater around the center of the bed. Push one sleeve into the other, overlapping the two cuffs by about 3 in (7.6 cm). Pin and sew the cuffs together. Remove the pins.

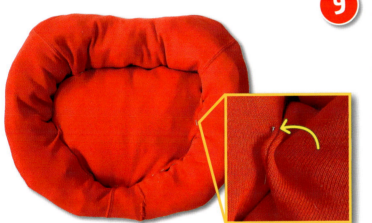

9 Now, ask an adult helper to help you pin the arms to the center cushion in about 10 places. In each pinned spot, sew about six big stitches that securely attach the arms to the center of the bed. Be sure to remove all the pins when you're done!

TIME FOR A NAP, BUSY BUNNY!

YUMMY BUNNY CARROT CAKE

A pet rabbit should mainly eat fresh hay, grass, and leafy greens. But as a special treat, your rabbit can eat some carrot or apple, and this **recipe** combines both—a delicious carrot cake with apple frosting!

You will need

- A handful of parsley leaves
- ¼ apple, cored and peeled
- A carrot
- A dark-green cabbage leaf
- An adult helper
- A sharp knife
- A grater
- A small microwaveable bowl
- Measuring spoons
- Water
- A spoon
- ¼ cup rolled oats
- A blender
- A 3 in (7.5 cm) wide round, metal cookie cutter
- A baking pan

1 While you wash and dry the apple and the vegetables, ask your adult helper to **preheat** the oven to 350°F (177°C).

2 Next, ask your helper to chop the parsley into small pieces with a sharp knife. Then, have your helper grate the apple and carrot.

3 Put the grated apple into the small bowl with 2 teaspoons of water, and ask your adult helper to microwave it for 90 seconds. Carefully mash the cooked apple with a spoon until it is smooth and soft. Allow to cool.

4 Put 1 tablespoon of chopped parsley, the cabbage leaf, the oats, and 3 tbsp of grated carrot into the blender. Ask your adult helper to help you blend the mixture until it is soft and crumbly.

5 Place your cookie cutter shape onto the baking pan. Spoon the mixture into the cookie cutter and press it down.

6 Ask your helper to bake the cake for 15 minutes. Allow it to cool completely, and then gently push the cake out of the cookie cutter with your fingers.

7 With the spoon, spread the mashed apple onto the cake as though it is frosting.

8 Finally, decorate the top of the cake with a teaspoon of grated carrot.

HAPPY MUNCHING, BUNNY!

Remember! Make this cake for your rabbit as a special treat only.

BUILD A BUNNY MAZE

Wild rabbits dig underground homes called **burrows**. A burrow may have many tunnels, small rooms, and entrances. Make a cardboard maze that will give your busy bunny a chance to hide and play like its wild relatives.

You will need

- A yardstick
- A thick, black marker
- 10 pieces of corrugated cardboard that are at least 24 in (61 cm) by 16 in (40.6 cm)
- An adult helper
- Scissors
- A ruler
- A sheet of paper
- A plate that's about 8 in (20.3 cm) across

These instructions show you how to make a maze for a smaller bunny. If you have a large rabbit, you will need to make the maze pieces larger.

1 Begin by measuring five rectangles of cardboard that are 24 in (61 cm) long and 12 in (30.5 cm) high. Ask an adult helper to cut them out.

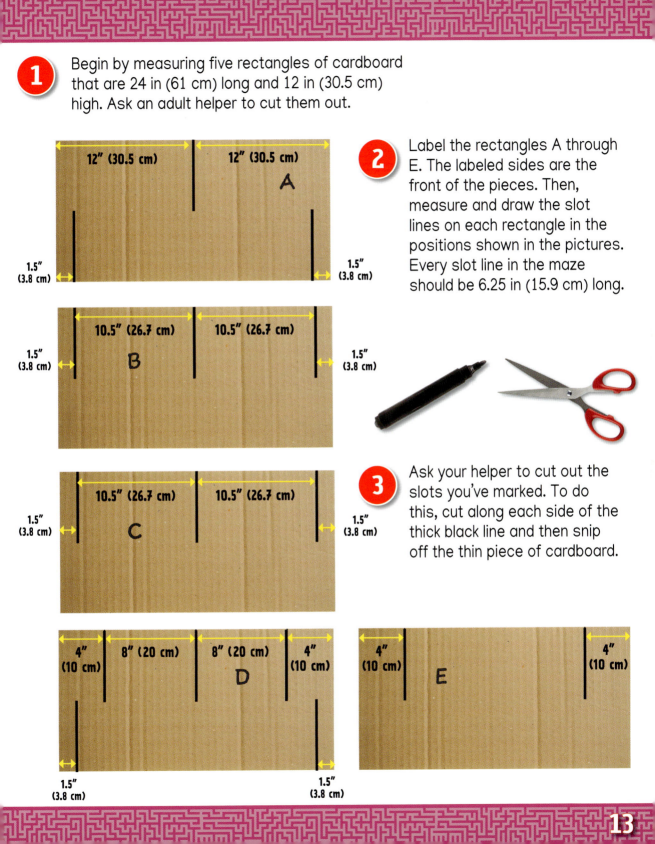

2 Label the rectangles A through E. The labeled sides are the front of the pieces. Then, measure and draw the slot lines on each rectangle in the positions shown in the pictures. Every slot line in the maze should be 6.25 in (15.9 cm) long.

3 Ask your helper to cut out the slots you've marked. To do this, cut along each side of the thick black line and then snip off the thin piece of cardboard.

12" (30.5 cm)   12" (30.5 cm)   A
1.5" (3.8 cm)   1.5" (3.8 cm)

10.5" (26.7 cm)   10.5" (26.7 cm)   B
1.5" (3.8 cm)   1.5" (3.8 cm)

10.5" (26.7 cm)   10.5" (26.7 cm)   C
1.5" (3.8 cm)   1.5" (3.8 cm)

4" (10 cm)   8" (20 cm)   8" (20 cm)   4" (10 cm)   D
1.5" (3.8 cm)   1.5" (3.8 cm)

4" (10 cm)   E   4" (10 cm)

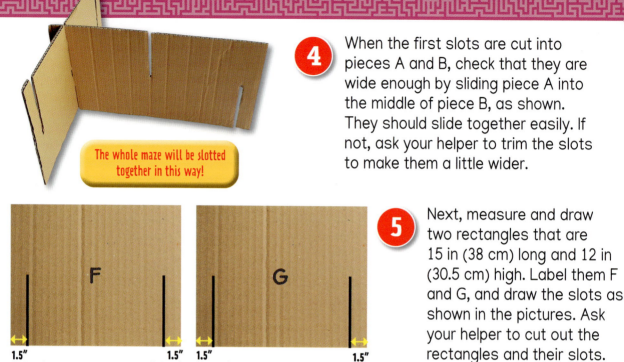

4 When the first slots are cut into pieces A and B, check that they are wide enough by sliding piece A into the middle of piece B, as shown. They should slide together easily. If not, ask your helper to trim the slots to make them a little wider.

The whole maze will be slotted together in this way!

F

1.5"
(3.8 cm)

1.5"
(3.8 cm)

G

1.5"
(3.8 cm)

1.5"
(3.8 cm)

5 Next, measure and draw two rectangles that are 15 in (38 cm) long and 12 in (30.5 cm) high. Label them F and G, and draw the slots as shown in the pictures. Ask your helper to cut out the rectangles and their slots.

H

10.5"
(26.7 cm)

1.5"
(3.8 cm)

5"
(12.7 cm)

6 Measure a rectangle that's 17 in (43 cm) long and 12 in (30.5 cm) high. Label this piece H, draw on the slots as shown, and have your helper cut out the rectangle and slots.

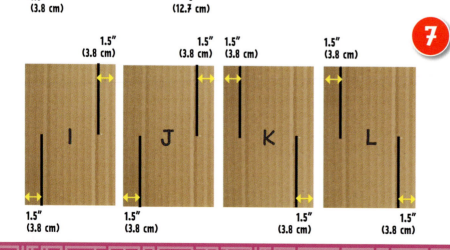

1.5"
(3.8 cm)

1.5"
(3.8 cm)

1.5"
(3.8 cm)

1.5"
(3.8 cm)

I

J

K

L

1.5"
(3.8 cm)

1.5"
(3.8 cm)

1.5"
(3.8 cm)

1.5"
(3.8 cm)

7 Now, measure four pieces of cardboard that are 8 in (20.3 cm) wide and 12 in (30.5 cm) high. Label them I through L. Draw the slots as shown, and have your helper cut them out.

8 Finally, measure a piece of cardboard that's 14 in (35.5 cm) wide and 16 in (40.6 cm) high. Label this piece M, draw the slots and a pointed roof, and then have your helper do all the cutting.

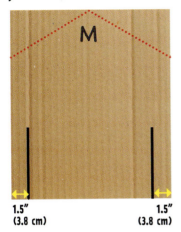

1.5"
(3.8 cm)   **1.5"**
               (3.8 cm)

9 On a sheet of paper, measure, draw, and cut out a door shape to use as a **template**. It should be 8 in (20.3 cm) high and 6 in (15.2 cm) wide.

10 On pieces A, D, E, and H, trace around the door template in the positions shown. On pieces B, C, and M, draw circles that are about 6 in (15.2 cm) wide. Ask your helper to cut out the doors and circular windows. You are now ready to assemble the maze.

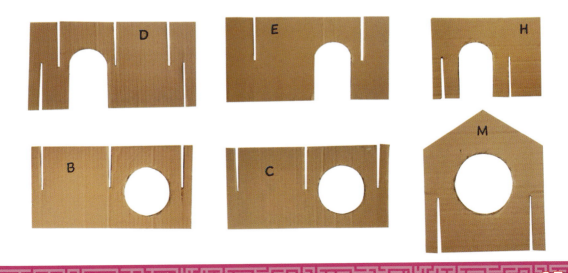

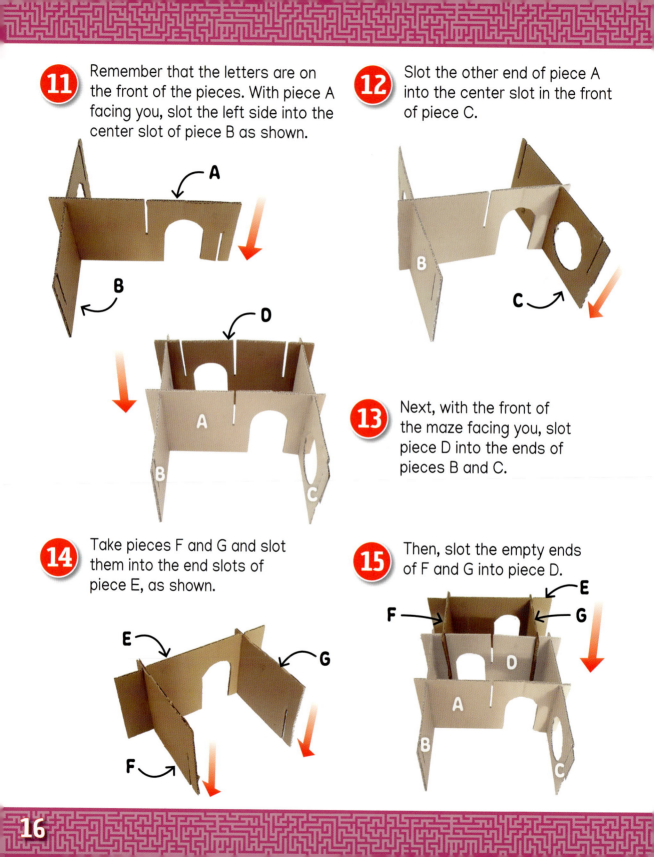

11 Remember that the letters are on the front of the pieces. With piece A facing you, slot the left side into the center slot of piece B as shown.

12 Slot the other end of piece A into the center slot in the front of piece C.

13 Next, with the front of the maze facing you, slot piece D into the ends of pieces B and C.

14 Take pieces F and G and slot them into the end slots of piece E, as shown.

15 Then, slot the empty ends of F and G into piece D.

16 Now, slot piece H into the middle slots of pieces A and D at the center of the maze. The front of piece H should be facing toward piece B.

17 Take piece I and slot it into the empty slot at the end of piece B. Then, slot piece J into the other end of piece I, as shown.

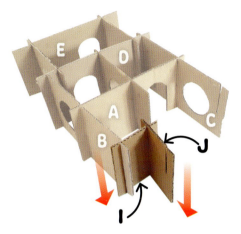

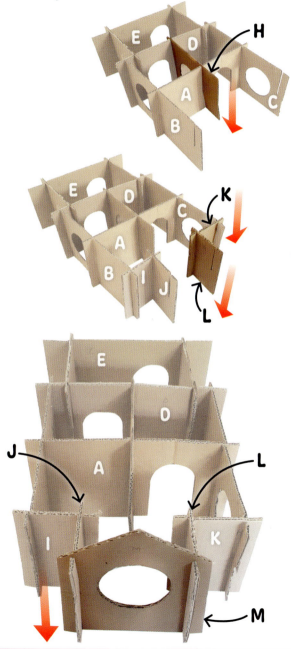

18 Slot piece K into the empty end of piece C. Then, slot piece L into the other end of piece K, as shown.

19 Finally, slot the sides of piece M into the empty parts on pieces J and L. Your maze is complete!

Show your bunny the door in the back (piece E) and see if they can find their way to the front (piece M). Put some treats into the maze to make it even more fun!

IT'S AN A-MAZE-ING BUNNY BOX!

CUTE CARROT HAT

Does your bunny chomp on any carrot it can get its paws on? Some say you are what you eat! Have fun making this adorable carrot hat. Then, pop the hat onto your rabbit's head and have a funny bunny **photoshoot**!

You will need

- Tracing paper
- A pencil
- Scissors
- A sheet of orange craft foam
- 5 green pipe cleaners
- Tacky glue
- 2 binder clips or paper clips

Never leave your rabbit alone when it is wearing the hat, and do not allow your rabbit to chew the hat.

18

 1 To make a template for the hat, begin by tracing the shape from this page onto the tracing paper. Cut out the template.

2 Place the template onto the foam and trace around it with a pencil. Carefully cut out the foam shape. Repeat to make a second foam shape like the first one.

3 To make the leafy carrot tops, cut the pipe cleaners in half.

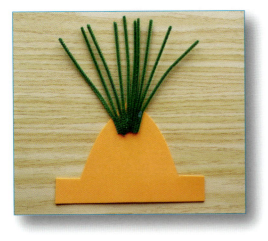

 4 Lay one of the foam pieces flat. Then, glue the pipe cleaners to the foam so that about 1 in (2.5 cm) of the pipe cleaner is on the point of the hat and the rest sticks up from the top. Allow the glue to dry.

 5 Now, use the tacky glue to stick the pieces of foam together by overlapping the tabs, as shown.

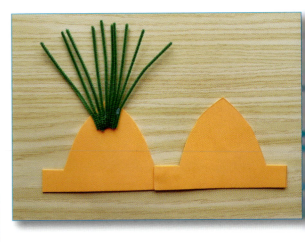

6 Then, glue the other side tabs together. The pipe cleaners should now be on the inside of the hat. Use the clips to hold the tabs together until the glue dries.

 Finally, bring the two points of the hat together and glue them with the pipe cleaners sandwiched between them. Allow the glue to dry.

8 Gently place the hat on your bunny's head. Its ears should fit through either side of the hat.

 Dress up your bunny for only a few minutes and only if it doesn't seem upset.

THAT'S ONE
COOL CARROT!

TOP TIPS FOR A HEALTHY, HAPPY BUNNY!

Being a **responsible** rabbit owner is all about keeping your pet healthy. Here are 10 tips to help you take care of your busy bunny.

1 Your pet rabbit needs a clean space with a place to hide so it can feel safe.

2 Clean your rabbit's space at least once a week. When you do, leave behind a little dirty bedding so it still smells like home to your bunny.

3 Keep your rabbit's water bottle or bowl clean and filled with fresh water.

4 Rabbits produce a special type of soft poop, which they eat straight from their bottoms! This helps your rabbit get more goodness from its food.

5 Don't overfeed your rabbit, and always ask your vet for advice about the best kinds of food.

6 Toys don't have to be expensive. Let your rabbit play with shredded paper, paper bags, or toilet paper tubes.

7 Rabbits chew. Keep all electrical wires away from your pet.

8 Rabbits are **sociable** animals and naturally live in big groups. If you can share your home with two or more rabbits, do!

9 Gently hold and pet your rabbit each day. To make sure your rabbit feels safe, hold it with all four feet against your body. Never put your rabbit onto its back.

10 A rabbit may live for 8 to 12 years. Be sure you are prepared to care for your pet for all this time.

GLOSSARY

accessory a thing that can be added to something else to make it more useful or attractive

active moving around a lot and getting plenty of exercise

burrows underground homes dug by wild rabbits

foraging looking for food in the wild

maze a puzzle-like group of paths, tunnels, or rooms that a person or animal must find their way through

photoshoot an occasion when a photographer takes lots of photos of the same person or animal

preheat to switch on and heat up an oven before putting food into it

recipe a set of instructions for making a particular dish or type of food

recycle to turn something old and unwanted into something new

responsible caring, trustworthy, and in charge

sociable likely to do well when interacting with others

template a shape that can be used for drawing and cutting around

INDEX

READ MORE

Foran, Jill and Katie Gillespie. *Rabbit (Pets We Love).* New York: AV2 by Weigl, 2020.

Yates, Jane. *Terrific Bunny Crafts (Get Crafty with Pets!).* New York: The Rosen Publishing Group, 2019.

LEARN MORE ONLINE

1. Go to **www.factsurfer.com**

2. Enter "**Crafting Bunny**" into the search box.

3. Click on the cover of this book to see a list of websites.

ABOUT THE AUTHOR

Ruth Owen has been developing and writing children's books for more than 10 years. She lives in Cornwall, England, just minutes from the ocean. Ruth has enjoyed being a parent to lots of rabbits over the years, including Lydia, Chloé, Hucknall, Arnold, Barry, and Hazel.